Color Me Furious!

Hilarious Sports Meltdowns for Passionate Fans

Welcome to "Color Me Furious: Hilarious Sports Meltdowns for Passionate Fans"! This unique coloring book is dedicated to all the passionate sports-watching guys out there who can't help but get a little carried away with their emotions during the game. We understand that cheering for your favorite team can sometimes lead to hilarious outbursts and over-the-top reactions, and that's exactly what this coloring book celebrates.

Inside these pages, you'll find a collection of comical illustrations capturing the essence of those moments when a fan's sports rage takes over. From the infamous referee calls that drive you crazy to the heart-stopping last-second shots that make you jump off the couch, each page is designed to bring a smile to your face and provide a lighthearted outlet for your sports-related frustrations.

As you grab your coloring tools and immerse yourself in these pages, remember that this book is all about embracing the joy and absurdity of being an overly passionate sports fan. Whether you're laughing at a missed goal, mimicking a coach's wild expressions, or playfully poking fun at your own overreactions, let this coloring book be a reminder that sports are meant to be enjoyed, even in the midst of your fervent emotions.

"Color Me Furious" brings a sense of humor and light-heartedness to your sports-watching experiences. Remember, it's all in good fun, and at the end of the day, it's the love for the game that truly matters.

Enjoy the journey and embrace your inner sports enthusiast with "Color Me Furious: Hilarious Sports Meltdowns for Passionate Fans"!